From My Eyes……….

…….Community Memoirs

From My Eyes.......

From My Eyes

(Community Memoirs)

By

Khalid El Bey

.

DEYEL PUBLISHING COMPANY

217 WEST KENNEDY STREET,

SYRACUSE, NEW YORK [13205]

CREATIVE RESEARCH SOCIETY

SYRACUSE, NEW YORK

From My Eyes.......

ISBN: 978-0615738307

Printed 2012

For information: www.khalidelbey.com

Cover illustration by Khalid El Bey

Published by

DEYEL PUBLISHING

217 West Kennedy Street, Syracuse, New York [13205]

CREATIVE RESEARCH SOCIETY

Syracuse New York

Printed in the United States of America.

Table of Contents

Chapter	Page
Dedication	6
Acknowledgements	7
Introduction	8
2012	14
A Question of Ethics	20
A New Standard	25
What is an African American	30
American Gestapo	35
An Educational Revolution	43
And Then There was Light	48
Calling A Spade A Spade	52
Coming to America	57
Day of Reckoning	62
Free Expression	67
Syracuse: The New South?	73
Love Lost	78
Poverty Pimps	83
Racism v. Prejudice	88
Set Up to Fail	93
Tea Party; Oh Yeah?	99
The Matrix	104
Werewolves	109
A New Dawn	113
What's Truly Valuable	120
When Our Protectors Become Criminals	127
Who's Responsible	132
Syracuse: An Actual Wonderland	137
From the Author	147

Dedication

This book is dedicated, particularly to the African American community in the City of Syracuse (New York), and generally to all similar communities throughout the world.

It is my hope that the reader realizes the undertone of the articles herein, and thereby be empowered to make positive changes that he or she deems a necessity in his or her community.

𝕬𝖈𝖐𝖓𝖔𝖜𝖑𝖊𝖉𝖌𝖊𝖒𝖊𝖓𝖙𝖘

I would like to give a special thanks to Mr. Dave McCleary, Publisher of CNY Vision Newspaper, for allowing me an opportunity to share my ideas and opinions in his newspaper; for absent said opportunity, this book would not exist.

I would also like to thank many of you, the readers throughout the Syracuse community, for your positive feedback and expressed appreciation for what I had to say.

-   Khalid Bey

Introduction

One Friday morning, we were in a board meeting for the CNY Vision newspaper, and one of the board members suggested that CNY Vision should be a paper that causes our people to think.

That statement has stuck with me since it was made, and so I endeavored, with each article that I wrote, to cause people to do exactly that.

While thinking about our community and its condition, I wondered what I could do (personally) to contribute to the improvement of my neighborhood and my city. I asked myself, "What are three important 'virtues' that I could establish as principles (for me) to follow?

It was these questions that cause me to write these articles, and to eventually compile them into this book.

Below are three virtues by which I am learning to live and my reasons for living by them:

1) Courtesy: Never seek personal gain at the expense of another.

- No one likes to be taken advantage of in any way. Example: I am a man who seeks financial gain by manipulating Women. As my financial condition improves, the Woman's weakens. Such an action by me could bring on repercussions that I may not wish to experience.

Though others may attempt to take advantage of me, I remain disciplined; never attempting to gain at their expense. Often a person who is taken for granted feels victimized and this is understandable; but to me, a portion of the responsibility for my being taken advantage of falls on me, because I had a choice in the matter (to engage the "wrong" party). From this experience, I learn to use discrimination in choosing who to engage. It provides less stress "for me", to simply count my losses, and move on, thereby reducing or eliminating the chance for further repercussions.

2) Honesty: Do your best to remain objective, even in personal situations

  - I mentioned before in one of my articles that America promotes self-determinism. Even for something as simple as exaggeration, there could be backlash. For example: It may appear harmless for me to tell someone that I made $50K per year, when the truth is, I actually make only $18K per year. I "stretch the truth" a bit (or a lot) so to improve my "position" amongst a particular crowd; but chances are, someone could come across my check stub, or get hired at the same place where I work and find out that I lied. Some may say "so what"; but if improving my position in the eyes of my peers was so important that I had to lie about how much money I made, then it may be just as important (to me) for them to not find out that I lied. In this respect, embarrassment is the backlash.

Simply stating the truth, or not saying anything at all assures a much more comfortable outcome.

3) Selflessness: Seek the greater good of the group.

   - I might be a person who is concerned about my progress and the progress of my family, and rightfully so; but, it's very dangerous to be a rich man in the midst of poor people.....robbery or burglary could be a likely outcome.

If I worked to improve the workforce in my community, helped to create opportunities for small businesses, which over time, improved the economic climate in my community, robbery or burglary is less likely to happen, because of an abundance of economic prosperity throughout the area in which I live. In this condition, I could live a lot more comfortably as a rich man, with less concern for mischief.

In my opinion, there should be a blend of egoism or self-preservation and utilitarianism or group thinking. It is very difficult to provide solutions for someone, that one hasn't found for him/herself. Discovering how to preserve one's self gives you the ability to teach others to do the same.

One does not have to always volunteer large amounts of time or give away their life savings to the homeless in order to contribute to the general well being of their community. All that is required is that we work on improving ourselves, for there is no better contribution that one could make.

These are not at all rules for others to follow necessarily, but are instead an example of the personal virtues by which I try to live. What are yours?

It is my hope that this book provides the reader insight, that he or she may better handle our community's struggles and thereby improve the quality of life for him/herself and others.

-*Khalid El Bey*
Author

2012

The release of the movie 2012 had generated a lot of dialog about whether such cataclysmic events are possible, or worse, if it's probable that these events would really take place on the Winter Solstice (December 21st) of 2012. Science says that such dynamic events takes place periodically, as a result of years and years of accumulated damage to the Earth and its atmosphere; that after a while, the Earth does what is necessary to cleanse itself.....to begin anew. Though such an idea appears to be pretty well supported, even in biblical lore, some had argued that the events of 2012 would not bring the type of physical devastation to the Earth that was portrayed in the movie, but instead would bring changes of a different kind; a "paradigm shift", instead of a pole shift (maybe).

What would a 2012 paradigm shift be like in the City of Syracuse? Syracuse has been described in a number of ways by some of its younger inhabitants over the years; unprogressive, unwelcoming, boring, a retirement community to say the least. There has been noticeable change between the times of Lee Alexander to now. Many in the African American community reminisce about a time when there was an abundance of work opportunities, even for youth; when African American leaders like Clarence "Junie" Dunham and Charles Anderson worked hard to assure the people of our communities opportunities for inclusion.

Since those times, those leaders have been replaced by leaders of a different type. Aspirations to improve our community became opportunities for the execution of personal agendas, in the attempt to establish themselves as persons of significance. What once appeared to be the development of a "group conscious" deteriorated into a "self conscious". A lack of adequate representation over the past 8 to maybe even 16 years has left our community "sitting outside in the waiting room". So, many young adults from our community, as well as other communities set out to find greener pastures in places like Washington, D. C., Virginia, Charlotte, NC, and Atlanta, GA.

But then there was a spark of life. An organization of young and creative minds appeared on the scene. These new young leaders saw what has now been deemed the brain drain to be a serious problem, which required immediate attention. The organizers reached out to their old leadership, and won their support. Since then, 40 Below, love them or hate them, had emerged offering a new direction for the City of Syracuse; producing from within itself, young leaders who would go on to work for CenterState CEO, in local and state government, etc.

Unfortunately, the nature of the interactions between the young and the old isn't the same in the African American community. Our community custodians have yet to see the light, for they are still blinded by their own ambition. The African American community is lead by those who are stuck in the Civil Rights era; attempting use 1960's methods for tackling 2013 issues. Now before some of you begin feeling slighted, this is not at all a disregard for the sacrifices made by many during those times; but we can no longer try to fuel our future with actual or illusory triumphs of the past. Our community has been misled by individuals who have struggled for a long time to make a name for themselves. Today, some of these individuals feel as if "they have made it", and so, are not ready to past the torch.

An article that I wrote titled "Poverty Pimps" caused a disturbance like that of a tremor under the feet of a few of the aforementioned characters. Some even went as far to explain their position(s), with hopes of removing the light of interrogation from their faces. Sorry, no such luck.

Reportedly, a cataclysm like the one predicted by the Mayans is preceded by certain warnings, like a change in climate, and the awakening of recently dormant volcanoes. These warnings our world leaders should recognize or foresee such an oncoming disaster, so to prepare, not to withstand, but to adapt, and secure our future.

A message to our current misleaders: your inability to read the writings on the wall suggest that your vision is obscured and that your type of leadership has run out of style. The constant polluting and mishandling of the Earth and its resources overtime creates circumstances which force the Earth to shake it's self free of its polluters. Like the Earth, the African American community has now reached a point where it is now necessary that we shake ourselves free of our polluters. The toxin which has poisoned our system over the past several years has now pushed us to the point where the well being of even our immediate future is (clearly) in jeopardy. A cataclysm is upon us.

Syracuse, NY is currently experience such a paradigm shift, and there are many who welcome the coming change; but for those determined to withstand the shift, be prepared for your passage into oblivion; for there is clearly one reality that has escaped your thinking; that reality is that change is inevitable.

𝕬 𝕼𝖚𝖊𝖘𝖙𝖎𝖔𝖓 𝖔𝖋 𝕰𝖙𝖍𝖎𝖈𝖘

One of the more difficult subjects to tackle in our society is that of ethics. One of the reasons for this difficulty may lie in a lack of understanding of the difference between "ethics" and "morality". A lot of times when a person thinks that he is addressing ethics, he is in fact speaking about morals. Morals are the "rules of right or wrong" established by one's religion, nation, culture, family, etc. Ethics is <u>the study</u> of morals; <u>why</u> we may determine something to be right or wrong, or <u>what</u> makes it right or wrong.

There are many factors that contribute to the differences of opinion on what is considered right or wrong. For example, cultural relevance is one of the main factors that one would have to consider when labeling a behavior right or wrong.

What may be wrong in one culture could be the norm in another.

The United States is a nation that struggles with questions of ethics; with so many of its citizens being from hundreds of different cultural backgrounds, it's very hard to pin-down one morality. Of course, there are certain morals of a universal nature, which all cultures and religions may honor; like the idea that steeling is 'wrong'. Nevertheless, a good number of our ideas of morality differ.

In some communities, <u>new</u> cultures are developing. These new cultures, promote new standards that by popular opinion, are beneath what is socially acceptable in society. Amongst teens and young adults, the use of marijuana, embalming fluid (chippers, stick, butt naked, etc.), and other mind altering drugs has become a new standard by which individuals are accepted in certain circles. Add to the aforementioned behaviors that of violence, promiscuity and a lack of interest in education, and we have the makings of a real life Sodom and Gomorrah type culture right in the midst of our communities.

Unfortunately, peer and other social pressures wreak havoc on the minds of young teenagers, who are, for the first time, venturing out into the world to find and/or establish an identity separate from that of their families. These circle of influences become the isolated environments through which our young people's minds are developed. In this culture, there is a subconscious use of ethics, for young people are now challenging morality by asking: Why is smoking marijuana wrong? Why isn't murder an acceptable retaliation for being embarrassed? My sister has a Bachelor's Degree, but has no job; why should I care about getting an education?

From My Eyes.......

There are even some Adults who, in their attempt to be accepted by the younger crowd, will endeavor to justify questionable behavior, stating that an understanding of their condition is what is needed; what these same adults have not realized is that our youth live in the conditions that we've create for them.

We are approaching interesting times, where those who will be entrusted with the future of our communities will live a life influenced by a new culture of impotence. Disinterest and indifference will be a common characteristic. What then will become of our communities, our cities?

We adults have to become proactive in the fight against intellectual impotence. We have to realize that our kids are "our" life; that it is through them, that we can see the fruits of years and years of labor. We have to let them know, that while asking 'us' questions about morality is ok, their well being will ultimately be determined by how <u>they</u> judge themselves.

A New Standard

On Thursday, December 17, 2009, the CNY Vision Newspaper held its launch party celebrating its successful beginning here in Syracuse. This was a special occasion within the African American community, shared with many others who themselves thought that such a periodical, which focuses on issues effecting this particular community was long overdue.

Finally, a newspaper that provides a larger and more positive view of a community that is constantly presented in popular media as socially challenged, needy and violent. For the African American community, to experience news that is not influenced by stereo-types is very refreshing; but of course you cannot have a joyous occasion such as this, without a little rain.

The Post Standard was good enough to print a small article on its website (Syracuse.com) mentioning the launch of CNY Vision. This was a great thing, considering that news outlets seldom provide a platform for another; the CNY Vision though not a threat to the Post Standard, certainly taps into at least a small part of its readership. That understood, the Professionalism of the Post Standard was/is appreciated.

Unfortunately, the appreciation for the support of the Post Standard was disturbed by ignorant and racially motivated comments made by some of its readers immediately following the article. Now, for the many of us who have ever had the pleasure of reading some of the comments posted on Syracuse.com, we know all too well of the very offensive statements made by some of its readers. In fact, a good number of African Americans and Latinos refuse to visit the website or even read the Post Standard newspaper, stating that the executives of the news paper obviously support this type of negative content.

In their (the Post standard's) defense, the right to free speech I'm sure has a lot to do with why they may not censor offensive material. The problem though, is that some of the comments made after certain articles causes Syracuse.com to read like a Ku Klux Klan periodical.

I do not want what I am saying to be misunderstood, so let me state: this is not at all an attack on the Post Standard or Syracuse.com, but it is an attempt to bring attention to what has regenerated and could potentially increase serious racial tension throughout Central New York.

One thing the CNY Vision newspaper did not do was feed into the ignorance; but I must say that it is interesting that the African American community has been accused of being overly dependent and "a drain on the system"; yet when attempts are made to promote self-efficiency, we're separatist.

Apparently, some African Americans aren't the only ones trapped in a 1960's type of thinking.

These days, there are some within the African American community who possess a more futuristic type of thinking. They are of the thinking that the units of measurement used in the past are no longer adequate; that the standards that we as a community had been forced to "live up to" are no longer respectable. Today, we establish our own standards by which 'we' measure our successes.

America had begun changing a long time ago. Our country is culturally diverse, and this diversity is ultimately what makes America as attractive as it is to those wishing to take part in the American experience.

Believe it or not, there are African Americans who are no longer attempting to create feelings of guilt within whites for our past conflicts; we have moved far beyond that, and today certainly isn't yesterday.

As with any family, we all have those members that we may not be so proud of; whether their selling drugs in the inner city or committing murder in the suburbs. The whole of our communities should not have to bear the burden of an uncultured few.

Dave McCleary should remain proud of his achievements, not only with CNY Vision, but with the success of his other periodicals as well, and know that if no one else supports you, we will.

𝔚𝔥𝔞𝔱 𝔦𝔰 𝔞𝔫 𝔄𝔣𝔯𝔦𝔠𝔞𝔫 𝔄𝔪𝔢𝔯𝔦𝔠𝔞𝔫, 𝔢𝔵𝔞𝔠𝔱𝔩𝔶?

"When one takes the time to reflect on the reported aspirations of our founding fathers of this great nation, one can't help but to wonder: what happened? If freedom, justice and equality are the principle concepts of our nation, and if this great American experiment was a test of our willfulness to share in the responsibility and to compromise to assure that these three ideas together remain our chief cornerstone, then to date, we have failed miserably." (A quote from my book, "The African American Dilemma", which was published in 2009)

The idea of equality has been shamefully belittled, not in words, but certainly in the actions of those who swore to promote and uphold it. Efforts made during the civil rights movement in the 60's and times before, has led the charge in the attempts to eliminate bureaucratic racism; and though such great attempts have been made, African Americans and other minorities continuously struggle with inequality politically, in the workforce, and in American life in general.

For centuries, African Americans have struggle with identity, as a result of years and years of torment. So often when the issue of racial discrimination arises, it is said that African Americans are too sensitive; that slavery ended years ago, and that We (African Americans) should get over it and move on. I wonder though, if the psychological effects of slavery and/or the Civil Right Era have ever been taken into consideration?

While slavery has in fact ended, its philosophy lives on in the minds and actions of many. We see remnants of the Willie Lynch philosophy in the racial profiling of young African American men by white police officers, in an attempt to weaken their self confidence and "take their manhood". Without doubt, it can be said that racism is alive and well; that it is engrained in American culture and this is particularly recognizable in our racially segregated neighborhoods and places of employment.

From times not too far in our past, to the present, African Americans have made the attempt to adjust and "fit into" a society where we have been referred to as animals or sub-human; and have come across literature that has promoted our absolute extermination. Yet, we're too sensitive. Time and again, our efforts to stand before the rest of humanity with dignity are met by absolute disregard and disrespect.

What can be said of a person who, for the sake of appearing or sounding politically correct, speaks of fairness and equality, of equal opportunity and equal treatment; but in whose core there lies a distaste for people of a particular ethnic background due to fear and ignorance? I'll tell you what could be said: Nothing.

Who cares? Can African Americans really be expected to trust select individuals, who are clearly culturally ignorant, to "do what is right"? For years African American culture has been defined by everyone, but the African American. Even the title "African American" was no choice of ours. Both Africa and America are continents, not countries. Can "anyone" actually be African or American? A person living in Brazil is on the South American continent. If we are defined by the continent on which we inhabit, wouldn't a person in South American be American as well? I mean, if that's not the case; if nationality is not determined by the continent on which we live, then what 'is' the nationality of those living in the United States; United Statesians? (jokes)

To the "African American": We have readjusted or totally changed our walk, our speech, our dress and even our zip codes to satisfy the on-lookers. This is not to say that all African Americans should migrate back into the city; where you live is your choice, if it is in fact "your choice"; and not a mere reaction to societal influence.

It is necessary that, for the sake of our children, we seek to establish our own identity, our own culture, and our own worth. There is nothing wrong with honoring and appreciating who you are. Stop avoiding the celebration of your heritage, your bloodline, for the sake of keeping everyone else comfortable. I'm sure that when other cultures are planning their celebrations, they take into consideration how their love for themselves offends YOU.

𝕬merican 𝕲estapo

There is so much about our country that would cause any person to wonder: what type of people are we exactly? It is so convenient for Americans to say that we are the greatest people or that we are the most fair people on the planet; but then certain behaviors come into action that appear to contradict all that we believe about ourselves; like Arizona Law SB 1070.

It is amazing sometimes that there exists the type of mind(s) capable of producing some of the most reckless ideas. Arizona Law SB 1070 allows for Arizona Police to stop, search, and if they deem it necessary, arrest Latino People throughout the state of (Arizona). Under said law, Latinos are obligated to produce 'papers' showing that they are legally on American soil. If it is found that they are on American soil illegally, they will be criminally prosecuted, and eventually deported. The law also states that after conviction, and after a person found guilty is "released from imprisonment", they will be turned over to Federal Authorities. Does this mean that these individuals will serve time in the Arizona State Prisons first, before being deported? Are we really allowing this to happen? African Americans and Jews are still trying to get over the times when "we" were obligated to produce papers to show which plantation or concentration camp we belonged to; or to prove that we belonged to neither. Maybe the most frightening thing about this law is its use of Probable Cause as a means for determining "who" should be stopped and asked for identification papers.

The following is the definition of Probable Cause according to the Lectric Law Library:

Probable Cause

A reasonable belief that a person has committed a crime. The test the court of appeals employs to determine whether probable cause existed for purposes of arrest is whether facts and circumstances within the officer's knowledge are sufficient to warrant a prudent person to believe a suspect has committed, is committing, or is about to commit a crime. U.S. v. Puerta, 982 F.2d 1297, 1300 (9th Cir. 1992). In terms of seizure of items, probable cause merely requires that the facts available to the officer warrants a "man of reasonable caution" to conclude that certain items may be contraband or stolen property or useful as evidence of a crime. U.S. v. Dunn, 946 F.2d 615, 619 (9th Cir. 1991), cert. Denied, 112 S. Ct. 401 (1992).

It is undisputed that the Fourth Amendment, applicable to the states through the Fourteenth Amendment, prohibits an officer from making an arrest without probable cause. McKenzie v. Lamb,

738 F.2d 1005, 1007 (9th Cir. 1984). Probable cause exists when "the facts and circumstances within the arresting officer's knowledge are sufficient to warrant a prudent person to believe that a suspect has committed, is committing, or is about to commit a crime." United States v. Hoyos, 892 F.2d 1387, 1392 (9th Cir. 1989), cert. denied, 489 U.S. 825 (1990) (citing United States v. Greene, 783 F.2d 1364, 1367 (9th Cir. 1986), cert. denied, 476 U.S. 1185 (1986)).

When there are grounds for suspicion that a person has committed a crime or misdemeanor, and public justice and the good of the community require that the matter should be examined, there is said to be a probable cause for, making a charge against the accused, however malicious the intention of the accuser may have been. And probable cause will be presumed till the contrary appears. (http://www.lectlaw.com/def2/p089.htm)

To simplify, this one individual (Police Officer), by his knowledge and understanding, will determine if a person is <u>about</u> to commit a crime. Answer this for me: "HOW"? How can one determine whether a person is about to commit a crime? Are Police Officers now mind readers? For the person(s) who might in fact be preparing to commit a crime, but has no weapon; how are Police Officers to make such a determination? On what will such a determination be based? Probable Cause has to be one of "the most" unconstitutional practices in existence, yet, our political leaders have allowed for so many to be detained under this unlawful measure. ("the Ninth Amendment [US Constitution] has played a significant role in establishing a constitutional right to privacy." http://legal-dictionary.thefreedictionary.com/9th+Amendment)

When the statement is made by the Federal Courts regarding "rights retained by the people", they usually refer to the 9th Amendment of the US Constitution. For example, there is no mentioning in the US Constitution of a power possessed by the police to stop a person on the street "on a hunch". In fact, a person's freedom of locomotion is violated when a police officer stops their movement, for this right to move about freely is reserved by the people. This stoppage, according to law is considered "an arrest". With this understanding, one could come to realize that stopping an individual under Probable Cause could constitute an arrest under false pretenses.

The fact that a man or woman is a police officer does not automatically mean that they are without bias, nor does it mean that they have obtained any spectacular amount of emotional or desire control, which may provide them an ability to judge without bias. Americans should trust the thoroughness of probable cause about as much as we trust the fairness and competency of Adolf Hitler.

Shame on the Arizona Law makers who obviously lacked the foresight to determine the effects that such a law might have on those Latino-Americans "who are" Citizens of this great nation. Shame on any person of color who might think that the passing of this law in Arizona doesn't affect them. What if the same type of law is passed for would be illegal immigrants from Africa or Asia? Wouldn't every African American and Asian American be subject to the same type of treatment? We already know that [we] African Americans are still haunted by Jim Crow, and what's crazy is that today we feel the Jim Crow effect in the North more than African Americans do in the South.

Recently, a New York State Senator attempted to introduce a similar law for people of Arab descent. There is something very sinister brewing in this country. We need our political leaders to stand up and do what is right in order to prevent the very tyranny that the four fathers of this nation worked so hard to suppress. We cannot sit by and watch this disaster take place in Arizona, for this law affects every single freedom of every single person in these United States.

An Educational Revolution

In March of 1854 Philadelphia Pennsylvania, at the National Convention for the Red Men's Whig Party, a New York Tribune Newspaper Editor by the name of Horace Greeley would make moves that would change the United States forever.

No more would his newspaper discuss violence, crime, scandal, fruitless medical reports and the like; but would instead provide subject matter that promoted morality, dignity and intelligence. Horace Greeley had launched an educational revolution.

In a time when the morality of slavery came into question and attempts to prevent a civil war had failed, it was understood by some that what was needed was a change or evolution in the thinking of the people. Today, in 2013, this idea of a revolution against intellectual inertia or inactivity must be revisited.

For at least the past two decades, African American, and American culture in general, has been characterized by entertainment, recreation and violence. What developed into an innate need for fun, or for activities that provide pleasure, has become the sole motivation of many Americans. Any activity that causes strain or requires effort; an effort which may cause momentary discomfort, is undesirable. Many of us would forgo reading and physical exercise, for the night club and junk food.

In times such as these, where the ability and skill of every man and woman is called into question, there is no other solution, except education. President Obama has made his plea, that every American adult invest in themselves by getting involved in some school or trade program; he (President Obama) stated that education is the only true way out of poverty; and I agree.

Take this into consideration: The first thing that comes to mind when one hears the word poverty, is money; but what about intellectual poverty? Most Americans attend college to acquire a certain level of understanding about a particular area of study. This level of understanding ultimately determines our level of pay. What this suggests is that our capacity to earn money is directly related to what we know; so understandably, if we know nothing, we can earn nothing. Every money transaction that takes place anywhere in the world, if not for a physical product, is for some type of service that the service provider is capable of performing; key word: capable. In other words, each of us are paid according to what we know, for even if one earns money by providing a product, he or she obviously "knows" the value of said product and "know" that there's a market for the product.

The previous paragraph should make all of us aware of the fact that one's economic circumstances are a direct reflection of one's intellectual ability. If a person wishes to improve her economic condition, she will have to come to the understanding that one resource that she has that can be capitalized on is her own time and energy. She must realize that the investing of her time and energy into the development of her skills and ability could have long lasting benefits. Each of us possess an abundance of time and energy to invest; certainly more than the amount of money we might have to invest. An investment in one's mind is a lot more beneficial than investing in a car or house.

It is not my intent to suggest that home ownership or recreation shouldn't be desired. What I am saying is that the world is not powered by entertainment or recreation, but by the people who possess the know-how to market and promote entertainment and recreation.

There is nothing in the world that is more important or more needed than education, for education empowers us to earn a living, care for our families, to co-exist in our relationships, to function in structured environments, and to adapt when necessary. If you truly want to improve or change your circumstances, your community, or even the world, all you have to do is invest in mind, improve your thinking and thereby change the way you view it.

𝕴𝖙 𝖜𝖆𝖘 𝖔𝖓𝖈𝖊 𝖉𝖆𝖗𝖐. "𝕬𝖓𝖉 𝖙𝖍𝖊𝖓 𝖙𝖍𝖊𝖗𝖊 𝖜𝖆𝖘 𝕷𝖎𝖌𝖍𝖙"; 𝖇𝖚𝖙 𝖙𝖍𝖊𝖓 𝖎𝖙 𝖜𝖆𝖘 𝖉𝖆𝖗𝖐 𝖆𝖌𝖆𝖎𝖓.

I have to say that I am pleasantly surprised. After what seemed like an impossible battle, some of the more influential people in our community are actually beginning to work together. The contractors are constantly discussing ways of increasing the amount of business they acquire; they are meeting with community development corporations, and coming up with solutions. Said individuals are examples of the people living within our community who are willing to work together to make things better for themselves and others.

Early on, a number of community non profits joined forces in an attempt to maximize their efforts towards improving our community. South East Gateway CDC, the Dunbar Association,

Southwest Community Center, Concerned Citizens Action Program and Jubilee Homes partnered to form the Urban Relief Coalition, who in conjunction with CNY Works and a number of other agencies were successful at securing $ 3.7 Million grant from the federal government's Pathways out of Poverty Program.

It can be said that efforts to unify our community representatives has met with some success. It was my hope, as well as the hope of many others throughout our community, that this type of team work continued. I had to chuckle, because as I state often, "with everything that exist, there is an opposite". Unfortunately, it seems that the culprits have struck again. Using the demographics of poor communities, certain agencies acquired funds and then cut our communities out of the deal.

Despite the aforementioned, the effort to unify is still applauded. Do not get me wrong; there still remains a few community back-biters crawling around in the shadows. We have community, as well as political chameleons who still feel threatened by the young adults who are becoming more and more active in our neighborhoods. I have witnessed these characters standing with some of these young adults and speaking revolutionary ideas, but when amongst their own (older) peers or others who are not of our community, they seek to discredit those same young adults; brandishing their forked tongues like thirsty lizards. Tsk tsk people.

Despite those who by nature appear to be negative and destructive, I have witnessed small steps in a very progressive direction. We, as a community, have to be intelligent enough to see the BS coming from a mile away, and at the same time, be able to push past unwarranted mudslinging. There are "some" in our community who are sincere in their efforts to make our lives better; Men and Women who work very hard every day to improve our quality of life. It is because of their efforts that I can say with hope that one day we may see light at the end of the tunnel....one day.

Calling a spade a spade

As I walked through my community on the South Side, I stopped and asked a few people the following: What do you think of the leadership in the African American community?

The response(s):

"Does African American leadership exist?" Who are they? Where are they? If they do exist, they're terrible" said one South Side Resident.

"We don't have any", yelled one passerby.

"African American leadership? There is no African American leadership; and if there is, they're only concerned is preserving themselves", said another resident.

The article that I was initially planning to write for this week's issue had a totally different subject; but over the past week, I have been approached by numerous readers who suggested that I continue to do what they say should have been done a long time ago: expose those who have taken our community for granted and force a change in our community's leadership. As you can see, I'm not the only one who thinks that new leadership is needed.

When you get a chance, take a moment to look around your environment. Make note of the number of blighted properties and empty lots; see the joblessness, the wandering or lingering teen-agers with nothing to do; feel the tension and the sense of desperation in the air, and ask yourself, how did it get this far? Bear witness to the work of those who took up the responsibility of negotiating on our behalf.

These misleaders who have developed a habit of providing the community with less than half truths; misleaders who have become experts at constructing "wonderful air castles" and other beautiful structures that may be experienced in mind ONLY; never really even having the potential or support to materialize.

The times where we have whispered our dissatisfaction for our misleaders amongst only ourselves has passed. It is now time that we shout our disdain for our misleaders for all to hear. Take the south side for example: if you'd consider the lack of progress in certain parts of this area, and the ghostly presence of former representatives, one might assume that there has been a vacancy of office(s) on the city council for years.

Think about it: the African American community has had a four-headed representative on the city council in years past.........or did we? Usually, if it looks like a roast, smells like a roast and taste like a roast; it's a roast....except in this case. It certainly looked as if we might have had a shot at some inclusion, but apparently we were wrong.

There will be a lot of people who will grunt and moan about what I am writing, but in their minds they will know that everything that I have said is true. DISCLAIMER: If there was by chance 'something done' on the behalf of the community by some of our "representation", I apologize on behalf of 'all of us' throughout the African American community who missed it.

Instead of being offended (when in fact it is us who should be offended), try doing some real work on behalf of "all" of your constituents. Go figure that a person would be concerned about upsetting people by doing what is right.

To the people of the African American community: this is equally a call for you to step up as well. We can no longer afford to remain on the sidelines, grimacing and waving our pom-poms in anger. It is time that we get into the game. Join the ward committee(s) in your perspective area(s); get on someone's Board of Directors, attach yourself to a cause and help those whose methods for leading might be outdated. Imagine what the positive differences in our communities would be if we'd only turn our words into action.

Coming to America

What's the different between the African Americans in Syracuse, and the people who have recently migrated here from Africa? There is a language barrier; there may be a difference in style of dress; there is even a difference in culture. There may be a few more minor differences, but what does this mean?

If we were to eliminate some of the "layers", i.e. dress, cultural differences, etc., what would we have? Language, of course, would remain our greatest obstacle, but outside of that, how else are we different? Why is there a wedge between African Americans and Africans in this city?

To the African Americans: here we have a people who resemble "us", recently arriving to a strange land that they might have experienced on television, at best. Upon arrival, they had no real idea of what to expect, and some, if not all of them, probably had no clue about how cold snow really was.

Who better to get them acclimated to their new environment? Who better to inform them about the realities of this city, this country? Why would we not make an effort to meet and greet them, invite them into our world, and help them find their way?

The beautiful thing about the above idea is that while we were helping them in their transition, we could have simultaneously been learning about their culture, their language, and the like.

Let's be clear, the responsibility for the wedge between the abovementioned groups does not fall solely on the African American. To those individuals who recently relocated to Syracuse from Africa: why have you not reached out? Why have you stayed away from African American communities? Why do you turn your heads, or worse, drop your heads when you pass an African American in the street? Why do you choose to associate with other ethnic groups, but select not to associate with those who resemble you? It seems more intelligent to associate with 'everyone' as much as possible.

I do not want anyone to confuse what I am saying. This is not at all a statement to suggest that one ethnic group should not associate with another; but I am asking, who could better help you understand the "nature" of this society than the African American?

I've recently spoke to one person who move to American from Africa in the not too distant past, and he mentioned his surprise at how a couple of white police officers addressed him, pulling their guns on him and using racial epithets. We hear in the news and throughout our communities about the cultural insensitivity displayed by African American teenagers.

Until the situation is thoroughly handled, institutionalize, and blatant racial prejudice is very much alive. Imagine the confusion and discomfort experienced by a person to whom such disrespect and disregard totally contradicts all that they've heard or been told about our country. Imagine the feeling(s) of loneliness and/or isolation one must feel when attempting to make the transition into a fast paced, every man for himself type of environment; an environment filled with tension and desperation.

Some would be foolish enough to say that "they're from Africa; they've seen much harder times than we have. This is nothing for them." While it may be true that they might have experienced harder times than we, America provides an experience like no other.

We have to do a better job at understanding one another. We have to make an effort to become familiar; to bring our communities together and learn from each other. There is no telling what we might be able to accomplish as one voice. Imagine the possibilities.

Day of Reckoning

It is very hard for someone who has, over time, made his living off of fooling people, to cope with the idea of becoming insignificant. We've all seen those movies where a near criminal, who has taken advantage of some sort of system, is on the verge of being exposed. We've seen the acts of desperation performed by him to preserve his way of life; a way of life that has, up until this moment, been one of lies and deceit, supported by a history of vile secrets; the type of which, if ever brought to light, would mean the absolute annihilation of his name and reputation.

The audacity of such persons who, in their attempts to preserve only themselves, will sacrifice the whole of a people; constantly mistaking cleverness for intelligence, they use feeble 'strong arming tactics' to coerce individuals to "see things their way". Yes, I used the term coerce, because that's exactly what it is. The word: _coerce_ means *to compel by force, intimidation, or authority, esp. without regard for individual desire or volition.* (Dictionary.com) Findlaw.com defines coercion as *"the use of express or implied threats of violence or reprisal (as discharge from employment) or other intimidating behavior that puts a person in immediate fear of the consequences in order to compel that person to act against his or her will."* Coercion is a "Class A Misdemeanor" or a "Class D Felony", depending on the nature of the direct or implied threat.

What's interesting and very obvious about the aforementioned is that in such a situation, the culprit clearly has not thoroughly thought his plans through; hence my reason for labeling said plans as acts of desperation.

Syracuse certainly has within it, certain men and women who possess the power and influence to 'alter its climate', but it has its 'wanna-be(s)' as well; people who sit in their hovels, like crazed, delusional ego-maniacs, developing schemes for maintaining 'their position', and determining whose necks they will step on to do it. With every change that takes place they feel their grip on the community or city loosen, causing them to roam political hallways and streets like scavengers, with their noses to the ground trying to sniff out their next meal.

To the African American community: What are we to do, when no matter how many times we've forgiven persons for selling us short, or let them slide, by forgetting their past transgressions, they're never appreciative? Instead of thinking about the whole, they continue to display their conniving nature. We've all heard the story of the turtle and the scorpion.

Harsh words, I know, but as I stated in a previous article, let's just call a spade, a spade. Even now, with this very article, another appeal is being made; so allow me to re-state for the record: these are not my thoughts alone, but are instead the thoughts of many who see the wrong being done by those who claim to be doing what's right for our community.

Intelligence is defined as: *"having good understanding or a high mental capacity; quick to comprehend...displaying or characterized by quickness of understanding, sound thought, or good judgment."* (Dictionary.com) I and many others could probably point out at least six (6) areas within the meaning of this word, where the behavior of certain community vultures falls short. To behave in a certain way, all the while knowing that what you are doing is done at the expense of our community, clarifies for us your intent.

We all have to make a living in order to preserve our families, and this is of course, very noble; but it is when one goes "outside" of those more noble methods of self-preservation, by sabotaging the efforts made by others to do same, that the person in question has gone too far.

Get a grip, cleanse your thoughts, get control over the emotional color that haunts your mind, and view the world for the first time with clean eyes. See the calamity you've caused and repent; and maybe we'll forgive you.

Free Expression

What would man be, absent creativity? I'll tell you what he would be: naught, useless, nothing or without purpose. Creativity is that purposeful action that perpetuates all that is living. It (creativity) is that which is narrated in the first chapter of Genesis; it is **the cause** of the beginning; what is displayed in "**bereshith**".

In every aspect of life, we all bear witness to the wonders of creativity, whether performed by nature or Man. Everything from child birth, to the construction of skyscrapers, to the development of the newest technology or medicine; all that we see exist via creative expression.

What is it then that causes a man to suppress his creativity? Self doubt? Fear of ridicule or non acceptance? There are many contributing factors to a person's creative suppression (suppression, instead of expression).

For a long time, I had been involved in music and entertainment. To me, Hip Hop was only as defined by or truly demonstrated in the North East of the United States. Anything else wasn't Hip Hop (to me). I was totally biased against southern rap, or rap music from anywhere, other than New York, New Jersey, or Philadelphia.

It was only recently, that I've come to a more clear understanding of what it means to be (truly) creative, and the personal benefits one receives when being creative. This recent discovery caused me to reconsider my ideas about rappers outside of the tri-state area; understanding that what I and others are witnessing are their modes of expression. What must be realized though is the difference between true creativity, and the mere "reflecting" of another's creativity; or what is referred to in Hip Hop as "biting". Biting another's lyrics, their style, their delivery, their posture; this IS NOT creativity, but is instead a "cloning" of another's expression.

Nevertheless, the courage that it takes for one to "put himself on the line" by expressing his personal thoughts or feelings through music, paintings, novels, etc., is commendable. There is nothing more satisfying than living "in the midst" of one's creativity, for it is when we are "in that moment" that we experience true freedom. Absent this freedom of expression, what would the world be, except a place without ratio or proportion; a world of one tone, note or key, where the beauty of melody could not be realized. A world where the size, shape and color of objects would no longer contribute to its character.

Creativity provides the world that necessary 'difference', or contrast; that reasonable contradiction that allows the validation of all that is and is not. While reading this article, witness the aesthetic beauty of language and its fluidity and adaptability.

Many have asked me, if I am a poet? I reply, "no", certainly not with purposeful intent, but I AM a word spoken, traveling by breath through an intricate combination of paths or passages in which it is difficult to find one's way or to reach the exit; an exit from adversity and mere moments of satisfaction, in search of a longer, more sustaining peacefulness. Wow, that was poetic.

But what would this "peacefulness", this Utopia present us, but a world where all boundaries are blurred; where true racial acceptance and equality is achieved; where the cause or need for war no longer exist, and nations blend all efforts and resources to preserve our world's civilization. Now here I must be careful, less I be accused of promoting a one world government within a New World Order. Look at the contradiction though; we need free expression, with all of its contrast or differences, yet we seek a blend of all opposites, in search of a silence, so beautiful and harmonious.

It seems crazy to witness the beauty on both sides of an issue; to realize that even in the "in between" of an issue or in the conflict itself, there is beauty. It helps one to understand how each "side" has its supporters and nay-sayers. What may be required by both sides is an understanding of the opposite; an ability to see the necessity of both, and how each (opposite) provides a platform for the other to exist. Understandably, it is very hard to realize that Life itself is a "catch 22"; but it is through one's creative expression, that this constant contradiction (life) is put on display. Some say that it is such a gift, yet a curse to be alive, but who would change it? Certainly not me.

Is Syracuse the New South?

While sitting and contemplating what I would write for this week's edition of CNY Vision, I tried to identify something; anything that could be considered a major or progressive move within the African American community here in Syracuse. There has certainly been some movement; this CNY Vision Newspaper could be seen as a sign of progress. A deal reached between Clear Channel Communications and select community members to work together to save Power 620 (the lone Black radio format) might be seen as another sign of progress.

Mayor Miner's appointment of Frank Fowler as Chief of Police and Sharon Owens as Deputy Commissioner of the Department of Neighborhood and Business Development could be considered a sign of progress, but the praise for those appointments goes to the Mayor and those individuals for their personal efforts to improve our city.

In the two above paragraphs are displayed examples of individual and/or community progress; progress that I am certainly proud of; but how are we doing overall?

So many people, including some African Americans consider the subject of equal opportunity and racial equality 'old'. Said individuals refuse to be associated with anything that might be labeled "black", for fear of damaging their socio-economic and/or political 'positions'; citing that there's no need to isolate ourselves from everyone else. Some African Americans actually feel guilty for being associated with any sort of "black movement". This I find interesting for it is reminiscent of the old south, where those slaves residing in the house with their "masters" would refuse to do anything that might upset him (master). They would urge the slaves who appeared to go against the establishment to "stop being a fool; what's better than what we got here?" These same house bunnies would sometimes alert their masters that there was a plot taking place amongst the field hands, after which a slave's master would pat him on his head and say "good boy Toby, good boy".

So many of our people have made the transition from Kunta Kinte to "Toby". When around African Americans only, they talk as if they are about our progress, but disassociate themselves from us behind our backs.

What is the big deal? Why not associate with being Black? Think about it: is there any one thing that you could name that African Americans have done "together" in this city; can you name one issue that we have stuck to until the end? If not, you have to ask yourself, why not? Why can't we seem to find a common ground amongst ourselves? Why is it that when one or a few of us attempt to promote and/or establish a common issue, others amongst our community work hard to sabotage those efforts? Are we truly incapable of developing one vision, or are we still dealing with in-house backstabbers, who would sell their young to save themselves?

It's a little troubling when you think about it. I mean, it is very possible that some of these house hands really mean well; but a lack of foresight and an inability to separate personal instinct from group instinct causes their efforts for progress to become acts of separation and destruction.

I really mean no harm when making statements like the one made in the last paragraph. My intent is to speak directly, so to alert our Court Jesters of their behavior. We'd much rather them get a clue and shape up on their own, than to continue this public (verbal) caning; but for some reason, they don't seem to be getting the message.

Time and again, efforts to organize on behalf of the African American community are met with disdain. Some from within our community would have you believe that to even mention a "black agenda" is too radical or that it seems confrontational. It appears that our "new" leaders, whoever they are, need to let the Court Jesters know that we are not in the South, and that slavery has ended (as least physically). They need to know that we do not tap dance for food, or that we do not smile, shake hands and "pucker up" for acceptance. The days of the house servant have long gone. I've always been a field worker....a Nat Turner type myself........how about you?

𝕴𝖔𝖛𝖊 𝕷𝖔𝖘𝖙

African Americans and other minority groups encounter numerous obstacles in their attempts to realize the American dream. Haunted daily by America's past, as well as its current intolerableness, several minority groups, particularly African Americans continually express dissatisfaction with even today's circumstances.

Euclidian Geometry suggests in its first problem that "with everything that exists, there is an opposite". This idea, which expresses "casual determinism" or cause and effect, is very popular in American society. When considering one's condition, the object or the external circumstances cannot be assumed to be the absolute cause. What must be taken into consideration is the polar (opposite) of the object; i.e. "the subject" or the internal.....namely, you.

The current behavior of teenagers and young adults stems from their early childhood environment. To understand what appears to be a lack of love and compassion expressed by our youth, we'd have to go back to observe the level of love and compassion expressed between their Fathers and the Mothers.

While this topic certainly applies to all, regardless of ethnicity, my focus is on African American love.

There are many who would argue that the current mental condition of the African American is a result of years of slavery, and the reported atrocities experience by African Americans as a result of a philosophy for breaking a slave promoted by William Lynch; a slave owner from the West Indies. Take into account the self-deterministic ideology celebrated in American society, and you'd understand at least one of the causes of an ever increasing divorce rate.

From the beginning of their teen years, African American men and women are conditioned to be self-serving. This desire to preserve one's self over all else causes a man and/or a woman to become noncommittal; setting their relationships up for failure from the very beginning.

Within the minds of many lies a certain level of distrust for people (in general), but especially when it comes to matters of the heart. Many men and women, upon beginning a relationship, are immediately concerned about the probable infidelity of their mate. This idea creates within him or her an apprehensiveness, and sometimes even a fear of moving forward or committing him or herself 100%. This apprehension is noticed by the opposite person, who in turn becomes apprehensive him/herself. At this point a "stalemate" ensues, and the death of the relationship has already begun.

This "new" distrust that exist as a result of a "fear of loss and embarrassment", stemming from one's own self-generated illusion, creates within men and women a sense of desperation; causing them to lash out at one another with the worse type of hate and vindictiveness. All the while, their child sits and receives a crash course in how to effectively destroy a family.

Mom or Dad's dissatisfaction with one another causes either or both to become too irritable to reconcile, or to even tolerate their children; so the child is yelled at or pushed away for merely expressing a desire for attention.

One truism in America is that no one wants to claim even the smallest amount of responsibility for their circumstances. Everyone, in their quest for self-preservation, sacrifices the other guy with little to no conscious. I have sat in on or listened to many conversations regarding the various tribulations that people have endured; and all the while that there are telling their story, there is zero mentioning, or expressed concern for anyone else.

Where is the Love?

Poverty Pimps

The Irish community has Tom Young and Mathew Driscoll. The Italian community has Joe Nicoletti and Nick Demartino. The Asian community has a rising star in Tai Shaw. I could continue with the listing of the various community groups and their leaders, but there is one community in particular with which I am concerned: the African American community.

Who do 'WE' have representing us? Who's the champion for our community's interest?

I know of a couple of individuals who talk as if they are concerned about our interest as a whole, when in fact, they were really promoting themselves. They seek every opportunity to catch a crumb falling from the table, stepping on the necks of their communities in the process. How are we ever to stand-up and become self-efficient, with so many vultures hovering? Hey, what else can be expected? Poverty pimping is big business.

Throughout our history in the City of Syracuse, we have always had individuals who had been deemed our community's leaders by persons not living in our communities. These externally appointed characters ultimately become the "agents" of their appointers; gathering and reporting information about our communities to their "bosses".

In exchange for their services, these agents are afforded opportunities, like being appointed the Directors of non-profit organizations, or chosen to be the political representatives for our communities on the city council, the county legislature, or in government in general. Apparently, house n----s still exist.

Though these agents have been chosen on our behalf, their bosses will still ask on occasion,

From My Eyes.......

"Where are the leaders from the African American community"? My response: "I thought you chose them for us already".

Have you ever considered the various ways that money is generated on the backs of African Americans?

Politicians acquire glamorous jobs and reputations; drug and gun dealers sell to our community; more police officers are hired to deal with a lingering drug and "gang" problem; drug and gang task forces accumulate overtime; hospitals, pharmaceutical companies and other medical facilities make a killing; our local government attracts state and federal dollars; our area colleges and universities earn greater prestige and more state and federal money conducting "lab experiments"; a new church seems to pop up in our community ever month; clothing outlets, auto dealers, bars and night clubs, and on top of all of that, we have our own "in house" scavengers, creating non-profits out of thin air, all under the auspices of making our community better.

Before we can effectively tackle those external barriers, we have to first deal with our internal ills. It is time that we open our eyes and see our "community leaders" for what they really are. There is no need to name names, for these names have been mentioned many times, and "you" know exactly who you are.

For those of you who have tricked us, sold us out, or lead us to slaughter, it is time for you to retire. You've spent all these years creating a cushion for yourself on our backs, and at our expense. Though you have continually used and abused our communities, we've continually forgave you; offering an opportunity for you to better prove yourself; but all we've received in return was another slap in the face. We have turned the other cheek for the last time.

Under the title of community leader, you have sucked our communities dry. You've made it your business to remain informed, but have left our communities ignorant for fear that someone else might take your scraps. You've failed to groom or prepare those coming behind you to take your place. Our "community leaders" are so desperate to maintain their pseudo-significance, that they will lie and cheat one another for recognition and praise.

You have taken advantage of us long enough. Your time has come....can you hear the clock ticking?

Racism vs Prejudice

Why is it that so many people are afraid to discuss racism or racial prejudice? Is it possible that past thoughts or behaviors causes those afraid of tackling this subject to feel uncomfortable, even guilty? I have never been a part of any dialog, where the subject of racism or racial prejudice was discussed in such a way that it provided me a better understanding of why some people think and/or behave as they do.

Syracuse is a racially segregated city. The current separation of ethnic groups is not a creation of our generation, but instead a by-product of the thinking of past generations. Naturally, by being raised in a socially isolated environment, an individual could acquire the thinking and behavior of said environment. These acquired behaviors we display daily in our manners of expression, whenever we encounter someone of a different ethnicity.

When the above is thoroughly understood, one might draw the conclusion that "racism" could be more environmental. Nations affect laws which influences cultures, which influences communities, which influence families that ultimately shape the thinking of the individual. These "filters" produce in us a "narrow vision", allowing each of us the ability for experiencing mere portions of cultures different than our own. With this understanding, we may realize that our current ideas about and/or behaviors towards groups of different ethnicities, did not begin "in us", but was instead implanted in us. This appears to free us of the responsibility of being "racist", which in fact, it does......but, what about racial prejudice?

The word prejudice, in and of itself, does not necessarily denote racism. Prejudice is defined as an unfavorable opinion or feeling formed beforehand or without knowledge, thought, or reason (Dictionary.com). So a person could be prejudice against persons who are disabled, persons of a certain gender, or even against politicians and athletes.

While racism may indeed be environmental, prejudice is personal, because it is usually based on ignorance, fear or both. If a black man enters a room full of people of a different ethnic background, he may feel awkward. This feeling of awkwardness is based on ideas that the black man might have acquired over time, which may color his thoughts about the group he has encountered. Though the black man knows that he hasn't himself experienced this group, he allows the ideas he acquired via television, cultural biases, etc., to affect his judgment.

Though each and every one of us is certainly influenced by our environment, the choice to experience things different from ourselves is our own. This makes each of us responsible for our own personal prejudices. While it is a fact that all one knows is that which he/she experiences, our willingness or unwillingness to explore ultimately determines our level of understanding of different cultures and the like.

If you have ever, when encountering a person of a different ethnic background, "sized him/her up" based on ideas acquired as a result of environmental racism, then you are racially prejudice. This is a scary idea, because so many of us are guilty of the aforementioned behavior. Police Officers, Politicians, School Teachers, and other public servants need pay special attention, for their jobs causes them to encounter people of different backgrounds every day. This scenario could be likened to a person who may struggle with alcoholism; the first step towards a cure is to admit that there is a problem.

We cannot solve conflicts that exist as a result of racial prejudice by acting as if racism doesn't exist. Whether you're thinking and/or behavior is deliberate or habit, your racial prejudice is YOUR personal responsibility. If each of us would only own up to our responsibility, we might at the least be able to reduce racial ignorance, one person at a time.

Set Up To Fail

A man is arrested for a crime he has committed and is sentenced to 5 to 7 years in prison. He has two children by a woman that he is no longer with, and that he must cares for; but his choice(s) have landed him in a predicament that prevents him from contributing towards the care of his children.

Five years have passed and the man is released on parole; he is on parole for the remaining two years that he would've served in prison had he not been released. Once released, he is obligated to contact his assigned parole officer in a specific amount of time. He meets with his parole officer who tells him that he must find a job as soon as possible; that if he doesn't find work within a relatively short amount of time, he may be violated and sent back to prison. The Parole Officer then tells him that his driver's license has been taken away, and he doesn't know when he can have it restored. The Parole Officer tells him that he also has a 9 pm curfew and that if it is found that he misses curfew, he will be violated and sent back to prison.

When the Parolee gets home, he finds mail in his mailbox from the County Division of Family Courts. In the letter from the Family Court, it says that the Department of Social Services is seeking payments he owe for child support; payments that he couldn't make, because he was incarcerated. The letter further states that he must appear in Family Court to answer for what he owes, and failure to comply with the soon to be decided payment schedule will cause for his arrest for failure to pay child support.

Now, one absolute truth is that if this Parolee did not commit a crime, he would have been able to maintain his child support payments, and not be in danger of being locked in jail a second time. This would be the argument of many who are taxpayers, and community groups who work hard to either preserve and/or revitalize suffering neighborhoods. For the record, this is a very fair and practical argument.

Let's say that the experience in prison has caused the Parolee to realize how his choice of activity was the cause of his set back, and that his view of life is now much more progressive. He re-enters society with the intent of being more productive, but his circumstances being what they are makes it very difficult to gain his footing.

There's a good chance that the businesses that may consider hiring him, require him to have a valid driver's license, or he may simply need a car due to the distance of the job from his home. He has to report to his Parole Officer once a week, or for some, once a day, ultimately loosing time that could have been used to find work. He may have anywhere from 90 days to 6 months to find a job to avoid being violated. He has a 9 pm curfew, which could further reduce the amount of time he has to look for a job (retail places accept applications all day until they close). On top of all of that, Family Court is demanding money from him for past due child support payments that have accumulated up to $40, 000.

My question is, is it really possible for this individual to succeed? Without a doubt, there are some who are released from jail that do an excellent job at bouncing back; unfortunately every person isn't in possession of the same type of (mental) durability.

How is a man or woman expected to do what is required by parole or Family Court under said circumstances? No license, limited time (curfew, amount of time allowed before violation), and also one other thing that I haven't mentioned: the fact that times and therefore the required skill-set for today's jobs have changed. This person has been locked up for five years and has had no training. This obviously limits his choices for work.

Why is it that a person who is incarcerated has to submit a request to the court asking them to reduce the required amount of his support while he is in jail? The court knows that he is in jail, because it sent him there (though the parolee created his circumstances). Why can't the child support be reduced automatically as a result of incarceration? I know some would say, "Why should the kid suffer for his/her father's error?" Good point; but the kid suffers more from the father's absence (though also via the Father's actions). It's certainly a tough argument that I am making here, but at what point do we allow a person who wants to improve, the opportunity to do so?

Why obligate a person to find a job in what could very well have become an unfriendly job market?

Couldn't the parolee have the option of either finding work or getting into some kind of trade program, or both?

Considering the pressures a parolee encounters, it's no wonder recidivism is as high as it is. Please, do not confuse what I am saying here. I am not at all providing parolees with an excuse to be unproductive. This is for those "few" who have in fact learned their lesson, and who have come back into society with a totally different mindset from what they had possessed prior to incarceration.

It'll take a lot more than an article in a newspaper to create the types of changes needed to give those re-entering society a real chance at succeeding; but less we provide circumstances that makes their succeeding realistic, we send them into a whirlwind of repeat failure and disappointment that is sure to become a common occurrence in their lives.

Tea Party? Oh Yeah?

Have Americans become so comfortable, so complacent, that there is no longer a need to remain constantly aware of the happenings around us? Are we so preoccupied with our personal progress that we've forgotten the understanding that the progress of the whole is required to assure longevity of even our personal successes?

America has always had its issues with racial prejudice. Memories of past conflicts continue to haunt the minds of descendants of African Americans who were disenfranchised from as far back as the 1600s up to times as recent as today. I say "today", because the methods used to disenfranchise African Americans have changed over the years, and so, are more difficult to recognize.

So many in our society miss the subtle slaps in the face, due to a preoccupation with self preservation, but no one appears to miss more that African Americans. The subject of racial prejudice has always been an uncomfortable one. European and African Americans alike do their best to rationalize the questionable behavior or tactics of some, or even avoid subjects about racial conflict altogether. Unfortunately, we are now in a time where ignoring such behavior is no longer acceptable, and our progress as a nation depends on our ability to face this problem.

This is what I have to say to those of you who wish to act as if there isn't a problem: stop being a coward. Answer this: what is going on with President Obama? What has he done, that is any different from what was done by George W. Bush, Bill Clinton, or even FDR?

Is he a horrible President or can we be honest and talk about what is really happening? If you're fired up enough to voice negative opinions about Mr. Obama without any reasonable intent, why not just tell us all how you really feel?

Does anyone else, besides me, have an understanding of what the Boston Tea Party was, or at least who the victims of this "massacre" were?

Am I the only one who sees the racial implications behind the founding of the current "Tea Party"? Just the fact that a "Tea Party" that is reminiscent of the Boston Tea Party was formed should cause EVERYONE to raise their eyebrows.

"John Adams, who was a defense lawyer for the accused British soldiers, described the crowd as 'a motley rabble of saucy boys, Negroes and mulattos, Irish Teague, and outlandish-jack-tarrs."

(http://cghs.dadeschools.net/african-american/precivil/boston.htm)

Since when could a person or person(s) make threats on a President's life and not be paid a visit by the FBI? Knowing what the outcome of the Boston Tea Party was, we should understand that the forming of the Tea Party is suggestive of bringing harm to our President and African Americans in general. To the individual(s) who would say that what I am suggesting is untrue, don't talk behind closed doors; say it out loud, that way our community knows who we need to keep our eyes on.

Where are our human rights organizations? Where are all the noise making political hustlers, whose preference it is to choose those battles that pose less of a threat to their egg shell positions?

From My Eyes.......

Sarah Palin said on her web site, "Don't retreat, reload!!!" She had crosshairs on the states where 20 House Democrats are the representatives, and had a picture with cross hairs next to the President's face.

What are we missing? Did this really happening? Are African Americans really wrong to say that this type of behavior is allowed, because the President is an African American, and that prior to his presidency, any such behavior would have been met with absolute suppression?

Clearly African Americans aren't the only people not paying attention.

𝕿𝖍𝖊 𝕸𝖆𝖙𝖗𝖎𝖝?

Do human beings have purpose? This question has trampled the minds of many over the ages. Some of the greatest minds in philosophy and science like Descartes, Galileo and Newton worked tirelessly to make this determination or to discredit it.

It has been argued in the past that Man, much like the Universe, was merely a machine, without purpose, responding to physical stimuli. Some argue that Man's soul is what gives him purpose, just as God gives purpose to the Universe. This analogy suggests that God is to the Universe, what Man's soul is to his body.

When the above idea(s) are contemplated, one would realize that the question as to whether Man was merely a machine seems to be a valid one.

Think about your own existence; how do you function? Do you find that all circumstances in your life are determined by something eternal? Are you motivated by money, material possession, a desire for notoriety, ideas of self importance, or a need for power? Is your every thinking moment influenced by things, circumstances or people? (all of which are obviously external) Could not conditionings of all types be considered mechanical? Is your life a routine that varies very little, if at all? When you really think about it, human beings move and act just like machines (robots).

I thought this to be an interesting topic for a couple of reasons: 1) Most people have robotic thoughts and so would have never considered this idea without prompting, and 2) to determine whether such a condition could be the cause of our seemingly perpetual disappointment.

What exactly is a Matrix? Matrix is defined as: something that constitutes **the place or point** from which something else originates, takes form, or develops. Matrix is also synonymous with the word **master**. So a matrix can be like a template or a pattern by which thoughts, ideas, objects, etc. are fashioned.

Take into account the ideas of success that we acquire from our families, our friends and society in general. Each of these ideas or standards can be considered templates or rules by which we all must move (live). To many of us, anything to the contrary would be foreign, or considered radical, even extreme. Most of us, even without knowing, live within some social construct; some "idea world" generated by someone for a specific purpose.

Some of the structure provided by social engineering is needed, but too many of us are trapped in intellectually desolate states. Our inability to move or even see outside of the box severely compromises our abilities for adaptation. In this respect, change, innovation, and evolution become our enemy.

A Man who has low self-esteem and self doubt assumes failure even before an effort is made. This he does because he is trapped in a world (idea) where nothing works for him, that he isn't good enough, or smart enough. He's become accustomed to acquiring what he needs without labor, and when the ease by which he has acquired things tightens, he falls deep into a mode of depression. "Effort" is a stranger to him to the point where his mind and body (mechanics) are incapable of adjustment.

Yes, without a doubt, most human beings are in fact machines, living without reason, except to satisfy their more superficial needs. Capitalism has played a major role in the crystallizing of the minds and bodies of many. Unfortunately, the goal of "the few" is to keep the majority in this paralyzing position, and it is up to the lost majority to shake themselves loose. What will you do to improve your condition? Which are you, Man or machine?

𝔚erewolves

Uh oh; It seems that I may have ruffled the feathers of a few more individuals within our community. A colleague of mines always says: "if you throw a rock into a pack of wolves, the wolf it hits is the wolf who howls". When broad statements are made regarding the behavior of select individuals within our community, avoid "making yourself" the subject of discussion by expressing how the article offends you. If anything that is said offends you, you must be guilty.

It is no secret that our community, like all other communities need a little work. We all have our flaws, and some of us are working to correct them; but there are others who for some reason, act as if they are without flaws, or worse, that no one can see them. While it is not my intent to offend anyone, I am satisfied by the fact that you now know that "we see you", and maybe this slight exposure will cause you to do what is fair.

There are some people who read these articles, get offended and then call other individuals for "their" interpretation of something "I" might have said. How silly is that? Why not just call me? Who else can interpret them better? Better yet, how about we not call anyone and just do what is right, so that we are no longer the subject of any articles in the CNY Vision Newspaper or any other newspaper.

I sometimes find the behavior of some people amazing. It's like being caught read handed, with your hand in the cookie jar. There is immediate defense posturing and attempts to deflect the attention towards some more inconsequential matter. There are so many people who make the error of mistaking "cleverness" for "intelligence". Intelligence is not displayed by successfully sneaking around, knifing people in the back; nor is it displayed by spouting off information that "you believe to be true", absent any real research or experimentation. Intelligence is not automatically bestowed upon a person who receives a title of Director, President or the like; nevertheless, so many continue to believe that their efforts to further establish themselves are somehow intellectually superior and above the thinking of everyone else. It is unfortunate that there are some who feel that they are targeted by these articles, but you know what they say: turn on the lights, and not one, but all of the roaches scatter.

It is natural and understood that people in positions of leadership can make mistakes, but at least own up to them and make a sincere effort to correct them. If you're feeling guilty about something that was mentioned in the paper, check yourself; don't self destruct by calling around crying about it. If it was intended for people to know that "you" was the subject of an article, I would have simply stated your name. Instead, the attempt is to pass the message along in an inconspicuous way (smile).

We all have kinks that we are trying to hammer out. Some of us are better at hammering them out than others; but for those of you who appear to behave in this way voluntarily, you should be careful, for it will not be long before the very people you have deceived, figure out your tactics. Don't be upset by what is written in the paper, unless you can discredit it. So many are scraping around for significance and are sacrificing people constantly to establish some (significance). If anything appears to pose a challenge to their "position", their "standing", they'll lash out at you like a rabid wolf. Just watch them....you'll see.

A New Dawn

What can be said? One, a promising young man who's potential was beginning to unfold right before the eyes of many; the other, a 20 month old who's potential good in the world was, and will forever remain, unknown.

There are some things that need to be said, so I am going to take this opportunity to say what no one else wants to, or even knows to say.

First and foremost, to my community: we've had a lot of trouble over the years; senseless violence, untimely deaths. There has been a lot of finger pointing, and empty statements about community responsibility. We make the demand for more policing, arguing that police need to be more visible. We blame the City for not providing enough programming to keep "our kids" busy. We blame the schools for not being entertaining enough to keep our children interested in learning. Despite the fact that it is OUR community that suffers from all of the drop-outs, incarcerations and murders, we still seek to pawn our responsibility off on the next man, group or agency.

I understand the effects of the prison industrial complex as well, if not better than any other man or woman. I understand the dynamics within a poverty stricken community, where a sense of desperation, at times, sets in and causes one to "do what he/she has to" in order to feed his/her family and/or survive. I understand the feeling that no matter how hard you try to improve your condition(s) and maybe even the conditions of others, you fall short; each time validating the reality that you live in a society dominated by capitalistic self-servers, who's only concern is "the bottom line"; and this "bottom line", they maintain at "your" expense.

ALL of this we all understand, but there is one thing that we seem to be forgetting.....these are OUR children; not the Police Department's, not the City's, not the City School District's, nor the area Non Profits'. We need to stop looking for others to provide a solution for our problems or our failures. I know that many will be PISSED after reading these words, but that would only be another attempt to put the blame where it doesn't belong. My child (for example) is "my child". I am personally and immediately responsible for THAT Soul. There is no other human being more responsible for my child THAN ME! Period.

I will not act as if there aren't times when some (children) might "slip through the cracks"; but the larger portion of the kids who are merely warehoused, instead of nurtured (by their parents), and therefore, left to determine their way on their own, are the by-products of pseudo parenting and nothing else. So many parents are too caught up into trying to find their own way to a happy life, to be bothered with or to be attentive to their children. Newsflash! Your life is no longer "yours alone"; a large portion of your life now belongs to your children. Please, give them their share. When our children go off course, "We" have failed as parents, long before the larger community comes into play. There is no other Man or Woman, other than the parents in question, who should be expected to raise their Child; and if by chance the community contributes something positive in the way of said child's development, so be it.

I would like to point out one additional fact: what we refer to as Police are in essence a Para Military Organization; their "job" is "to police". Policing includes (besides defending the local, state and federal Charters/Constitutions) MAINTAINING ORDER, at all cost. Be careful when you make the demand for MORE POLICING; they (the Police) are not Social Workers, who offer counseling or offer youth programs as an alternative to incarceration. We cannot call on the Police, and then complain when the Police are doing what they were (specifically) trained to do.

Is the system balanced? Of course not. Are African American and other persons of color treated as equals? Of course not; and only a fool or trickster would say otherwise (so be aware). Nevertheless, "We" have to endeavor to establish the calm amidst the storm "ourselves". If we receive additional help, that's great; but We must take responsibility for how our children think, what they value, and how they behave.

We've had a lot of tough times (as a people), but we have no other choice at this moment than to stand up and restore order amongst our children and our families. We do not need anymore "armchair counselors" or "self-appointed" community leaders, mounting their soap box and gaining fame and notoriety at the expense of the lives of our children. Eliminate the fraud; stop screaming "stop the violence", if you have yet to gain control over "your own children", who YOU KNOW might very well be contributing to the chaos in our communities.

FATHERS: these are our Sons (and sometimes Daughters) adding to the confusion that has become common place in our neighborhoods. Let's save our children, and if you do not have a relationship with your son/daughter, it's not too late to begin building one.

MOTHERS: if the Father makes an effort, please allow him into your child's life. Stop allowing your personal dissatisfaction (with the failed relationship between you and the Father) to be your sole reason for denying the Father an opportunity to know his child(ren).

It must be understood that at this juncture; WE HAVE NO CHOICE, less our intent be to continue watching the lives of our children go unfulfilled, and their and our souls, be damned.

𝔚hat's 𝔗ruly 𝔙aluable?

I spend a lot of time either sitting or walking, and thinking about the condition of African Americans. As I am sure you have gathered, this is one of my greatest concerns. I think about our economic condition, our lack of political capital, the state of our teenagers and young adults; and I attempt to identify a cause. The more I thought about it, the more I realized that a person's condition has everything to do with where one focuses his attention.

There is no greater crisis in the African American community then the decay of the family unit. The decay of the family unit begins with the decay of the relationship between the Man and the Woman. The decay of the relationship begins with the ideas that one has about how a relationship should be, or what a relationship should be based on.

Many African Americans are so caught up in trying to keep up with the Jones' that they don't even realize the destruction they're causing in their lives. In the City of Syracuse the medium income is roughly $25,000 per year. There are people within our community who pay expensive car notes and very high mortgages; not to mention that they may eat out almost every day, spend hundreds per week on recreational activity, and we have yet to even factor in other responsibilities like the electric and gas bills or child support. All of this they do with an annual salary of $25,000 or less!

Believe it or not, money is not the main thing occupying the mind of most people; relationship is. Take the guy who grew up in a house where he had both parents; for whatever reason, he decides to take up the drug trade. He stands on a corner, risking his life and his freedom to earn what he could earn with a regular 9 to 5 occupation (with less risk, of course). He hustles all week, only to go to the mall and buy an expensive outfit, to go to the bar on Saturday to find a date, with the same women he sees in the bar every single week! How about the guy who makes an honest living; he might make $30, 000 annually, but his intent is no different from the last guy, for at the end of the week, he blows his hard earned money at a bar or some breakfast spot at 3 am in the morning.

Let us consider the woman who "believes" that it is the duty of the man to either work tirelessly or worse, put his life at risk in the street to ultimately spend every dime in the way that she suggests it should be spent; all the while contributing little or nothing to their "lifestyle". We can even consider the woman who does contribute. Between the two of them they may bring home $60, 000, but their appetite for comfort and luxury causes $60, 000 to spend like $10,000.

Too many people in our community focus their attention on things that they assume will bring them happiness; but these things are finite, and so, the happiness is only for the moment. It's kind of like a drug addict who constantly seeks another high, and this she does at all cost; but when the high comes down, she falls into a mode of depression and desperation; a mode where "everyone" is expendable; even her children.

There are women constantly seeking a mate based on what he can provide her financially. There are men who drive themselves insane trying to earn enough to attract and keep that same type of woman. There are men and women, who in their attempts to escape loneliness, will settle for even the worse type of treatment from their mate. All the while, each person is so lost in their own desperation, that the children are forgotten in the process. It's really crazy when you think about it; basically, everybody's "love" is for sale [hmmm].

I've realized that it's not that love was lost; what it is in fact is that the love was never there in the first place. Men and women attract to one another for a number of shallow reasons: looks, prestige, reputation, money, intimacy, etc. It's no wonder that the divorce rate is so high. You choose for all the above superficial reasons, not even realizing what you've done. Imagine purchasing a lamp from the furniture store. You take this lamp home, it's beautiful, and every day when you walk into your home, you take a moment to admire your lamp. As time goes on, you notice the lamp less and less, until one day the lamp becomes "furniture". Though the lamp has not gained a single flaw, you've become accustomed to seeing it every day to the point where there is no more excitement.

The same happens when you choose a mate for looks, money and the like. Money runs low, and looks will either go unnoticed or they will change with age. Bottom line, at the end of the day, all that you have left is conversation. This is when you actually meet the "real" person, who may be totally different from the person you initially started dating. In the end, if two people live with conflicting intent, the relationship is over. An inability on the part of many to see this reality is the cause of much disappointment in relationship(s). Eventually, the result could be the destruction of the family.

We have to check ourselves and re-examine that which we consider valuable. We have to do our best to eliminate the superficial, and not think so shallow; otherwise our lives will continue to be

filled with disappointment, neglect and regret.
Wake up people.

When Our Protectors Become Criminals

By now, I am sure that some of us have heard the story of Maparo Ramadhan, the gentleman from Burundi, Africa who relocated to Syracuse, New York in hopes of finding a better life. He was arrested in December of 2008 for domestic violence. When the time came for him to go before the judge, Ramadhan would not respond to the Deputies in the jail. Moments later 8 to 10 Deputies came in, and in the process of providing Ramadham "motivation to go to court", one of the Deputies broke his upper arm; giving him a compound fracture.

Now one thing that I will admit, is that in the midst of what might be a hostile situation, things happen; but there was no report of Ramadhan "fighting the police", but he was being resistant. I am pretty sure though that the Deputy who twisted his arm did so out of frustration or plain maliciousness (and that Deputy knows this as well).

What is even crazier about this story is the nurse, who after examining Ramadhan's arm said that "it was only bruised and swollen". Even though the Deputies present (one in particular) repeatedly recommended Ramadhan be taken to the hospital instead of the courtroom, a Sergeant who was present said that it was up to the nurse, and that they were two minutes away from seeing the judge; stating that "we're here now". Ramadhan's arm is now permanently disabled as a result of his injury.

Unfortunately in some cultures, domestic violence is not considered "wrong". While such behavior is not tolerated in the US, people coming here from other places may not know or even understand that. It becomes our responsibility to explain the difference. Ramadhan probably didn't even think he committed a crime.

Also, where he comes from, when people were arrested, and at some point removed from a jail cell, they would be killed. How could he know that he would not be killed when the Deputies came to get him? Further irresponsibility is shown by the officers providing a Swahili interpreter for a guy that speaks Kirundi.

My opinion: the responsibility for this incident falls on the officer who broke Ramadhan's arm and the incompetent nurse who stated that his disfigured arm was only bruised and swollen. This is a matter of ethics, and I am pretty sure that the Nurse violated numerous codes or regulations warranting her termination.

Maybe Ramadhan's fears make more sense than we've realized. 11 months earlier a young African

American woman dies in jail after begging for help for 14 hours. She died from a ruptured ectopic pregnancy. The US Department of Justice cited the county jail for poor medical treatment over 15 years ago. A few to several years back, an inmate somehow jumped from something in his cell, landing on his head in a successful suicide attempt. It appears that if you're arrested in Syracuse, you may not return home, just as those unfortunate individuals never returned home where Ramadhan comes from.

I really respect and appreciate John O'Brian and the Post Standard for running the story and posting the video on their site for all to see. I respect the New York Civil Liberties Union for stepping up. No sign of the organizations who supposedly represent African American interest.

I personally don't believe that this situation received enough attention. This kind of recklessness should not be tolerated amongst "Professionals". What will the County do to make this, the situation with the young woman who passed, and countless other questionable incidents, right? Maybe we should consider letters expressing our dissatisfaction with the handling of these situations. First nooses found in county facilities, then death and irreparable injury; and all of these incidents were affecting 'African' Americans, including Ramadhan. What are "We", the African Americans of this community supposed to think? Are all rules of ethics out of the window when it comes to "Us"?

Something else interesting to think about: out of almost 500 police officers on the City's police force, only about 20% live within the City. The rest are from suburb and rural towns, hired to work amongst a people that they might have experienced on the 6 o'clock news; it is no wonder police and community relations is so horrible.

Who's Responsible?

What are some of the issue facing the African American community? Education is number one. There is only so much that a person can do without an education. This statement about education does not only imply formal or higher education; but it also refers to general information. So much is happening in the city of Syracuse that many of us just aren't aware of. This lack of information prevents us from taking advantage of the many opportunities that might exist; opportunities for contractors and other entrepreneurs. Certainly, a formal education is key. So many of us may have taken the opportunity to be educated for granted, and a large number of us now regret the fact that we did not take our education more seriously. Obviously our lack of interest in education has led to our dissatisfaction with our personal progress, and circumstances for our young people will be much worse. The economic climate may be much different; much tougher. The increasing need for technological know-how will surely make demands on our adults of tomorrow; demands that they may not be able to satisfy, because of the lack of interest they might have had in education while they were in school. Needless to say, our community's future is in serious trouble.

Another issue affecting our community is the lack of jobs. Now this is a tricky one, because the fact is there are some jobs; but some of the jobs that are available may be viewed by those who are looking for work as beneath them. Hmmmm. The unfortunate reality is that there are many people who want jobs that they may not be qualified for. Without a doubt, we need more job creation; but we also need a whole lot of workforce development. Some of the people who may be looking for work, never really leave their front doorstep, because they know that they will more than likely be turned away, because of a lack of education or experience or both. My suggestion: for each day that a person who is out of work isn't searching for work, he or she should be investing in themselves in the way of some sort of education. Read the newspaper, take an online course, take advantage of one of the many education programs that exist in this city (Sydney Johnson Center, SUNY E. O. C., etc.) If no effort is made today, you cannot expect to be anywhere different tomorrow.

An obvious issue affecting our community is crime. Hopefully everyone is catching on, for each "issue" is a direct result of the previous (issue). It is either when a person doesn't have the means to support his or her family, or when the idea of working in a structured environment is unattractive to him or her, that he or she tries to find a quicker, and potentially more detrimental method of providing for his or her family. The real problem is that this individual has no concept of the future; every moment is a moment of desperation; as if life ends 'tomorrow'; so they have to get all that they can in as short an amount of time as possible. The problem with this type of thinking is that it can eventually become common-place in the mind of the individual(s) in question. Ultimately, their life remains one of dissatisfaction, disappointment and grief for themselves, and for the others whom their behavior may affect directly or indirectly. Believe it or not, this is a direct result of how one might have conducted himself while in the learning environment. Teenagers express a sense of urgency in every respect. From the time they enter a classroom, they are looking at the clock, counting down the time until the class is over. Their preoccupation with social issues (fashion, music, relationships, friends, etc) distracts them from what could guarantee them a productive adult life. After a while, this "urgent" mentality becomes "the place they reside", literally. They become trapped in a way of thinking that demands "everything immediately". This way of thinking is never corrected and is carried into their adult life. By this point, they began to realize that something has gone wrong. They come to the decision that they are too far gone, and urgency becomes desperation.

What must be realized is that our issues begin in the home. The children will not take education seriously if their parents do not. Parents have to become more involved in their children's education; we must understand that such is an investment into their future. Education is one sure way to reduce unemployment and crime. What are we going to do? Who is going to stand up and be responsible? "This" situation is definitely urgent.

Syracuse: An Actual Wonderland?

I was sitting and thinking about our city one day and I realized something interesting. We have some very interesting characters in Syracuse. I would like to take this opportunity to list some of these characters for the reader.

Have you ever been around people who were having a discussion about how horrible things are in our city? They speak so passionately about the dysfunction of our current leadership, offering suggestions for what a person in leadership 'should' do. These suggestions though, are never made to the "leader(s)" in question, but just amongst the small audience present for said discussion.

We are going to establish an identity for these backroom complainers and call them "Arm Chair

Activists". These are the types like those in the above example, who talk much, but do very little. Be wary of the Arm Chair Activists, for through manipulation they will attempt to get you fired up, imposing their personal opinions or feelings on you. They will attempt to cause you to dislike what "they" dislike, support what they support; boycott what they'd boycott. They will try to color your view of another individual or of some situation, for no real reason except that they may feel inadequate anytime they are around their Intended Target (IT), when the IT's name is mentioned, etc.

I've even heard of some of the questions that these Arm Chair Activists have asked about 'me'. One of the questions asked was, "Do you think that Khalid has compromised 'his voice', by taking the job position he currently holds?" Another statement was, "Khalid has softened up with his Vision articles; what's going on?" The truth about these two questions is that they are not questions in their true intent, but are in fact suggestive statements. These statements are meant to "color" my character in a way that causes the receiver of said statements to view me in a way that is similar to the presenter.

My reason for mentioning this is to demonstrate a couple of things: 1) it's an example to which I am intimately connected, and so, am very qualified to analyze, making it the best example to use; 2) since I am the subject of the above questions, I am the only person who is able to give an accurate response.

That being said, what then would be the intent of a person who voices those "concerns" to persons other than me? If these concerns were sincere, the individual(s) would have come directly to 'me' and voiced them. This is an example of the type of arm chair activism to which I am referring.

It is not my intent to confuse anyone. I am not letting any of our community misleaders (who from now on will be referred to as Court Jesters) off the hook. Our neighborhood foot shufflers and tap dancers are still out there, shucking and jiving throughout the city "on our behalf"; and many of these Arm Chair Activists who complain about these Court Jesters, keep them in power by voting into public office the same cast of characters, or characters who are 'cut from the same cloth' every election year.

Now, this next statement is going to upset a few people, so read at your own risk. I will take this time to paraphrase the publisher's disclaimer: the views and opinions expressed in this article are those of the author, and do not necessarily represent the views or opinions of CNY Vision.

That being said, I have a task for those of you who may read this article. When you get some time, drive or walk around and count the number of churches that are in your immediate community. Bottom line, churches make a lot of money. Churches throughout our city are buying up lots of property, but very few are developing with the intent of truly improving the communities wherein they are located. Instead they're seeking to make what the church has to offer more attractive, in order to draw more attendees. For some of these Ministers or from now on, "Soul Train Preachers", more attendees mean more money.

Now this message is not for those Ministers who "are" in fact developing with the intent of improving the community; but for the rest, who complain a lot, constantly voicing their opinions, and seek government (tax) dollars for expansion; when are YOU going to put in on this man?! When are you going to take some of the money you've accumulate from those community members who attend your church, and make good use of it by investing some of it back into the community?

Why can't community representatives seek to establish Community Benefits Agreements with churches that are looking to develop in their perspective neighborhoods? The church is a governing body itself. If its Citizens (congregation) are paying their taxes (tithes), it is only fair that their tax dollars be put to good use.

Last but not least are the Community Charlatans. These are the individuals who take advantage of every chance they get, to set up their soap box and whine about everything. This they do "on behalf of the community", but in actuality, their intent is to establish some significance for themselves. These are the worse types, for every bit of spotlight they receive is at the expense, or on the backs of some person or persons who have been the unfortunate victims of violence, economic struggle, political letdown and the like. They are so filled with emotion, that reason escapes them; and most of the time, though a lot of noise appears to have been made, there is no recognizable deliverable in the end.

It seems that no matter how hard we attempt to look to the positive within the African American community, there are still some not so positive things that require scrutiny. I am sure that this need for scrutiny doesn't only exist in our communities, but different communities have different issues.

For example, take a look around and ask yourself: has the socio-political position of African Americans living in Syracuse improved? Do African Americans even have a socio-political position?

One gentleman said to me that one's socio-political position is a direct reflection of his or her economic status; implying that an inability to "pay to play" is the reason why African Americans in general, struggle to improve their position.

Many throughout our community would still wonder: what have the leaders of our community been doing all of these years? A lot of African Americans lose faith in leadership, especially in situations where the topic of discussion appears "controversial". History has shown that in Syracuse, when controversial subjects of race, injustice, or general unfairness come up, leaders in the African American community duck and run in an attempt to avoid having to take a position and/or to make a comment about the issue(s).

There are maybe one and a half people who have stuck their necks out on the line, or at least made it look like they have; but once behind closed doors, they make deals on behalf of our communities; deals that we would never go for, but would further improve their personal position. This type of dealing they do under the guise of "strategy", referring to this shucking and jiving as "strategic".

How about we stop 'B-essing' everyone. Maybe the community needs to run an annual audit on the efforts of these cast of characters to determine their effectiveness; or, maybe these Arm Chair Activist, Court Jesters, Soul Train Preachers and Community Charlatans can forget about themselves, just for a second, and do something real.

Sometimes, life in Syracuse can help you to understand the confusion many have about the story of Alice in Wonderland; where she dreamed and search for greener pastures, stole from the Queen of Hearts, putting herself and others in jeopardy, only to find out in the end that all she desired, all that she searched for, was already in her possession. Just think.

About the Author

Khalid El Bey

Khalid El Bey, now an author of four books, with a fifth underway clearly has a lot to offer. Stating his recent realization of his passion for empowering others, Khalid Bey says "who would imagine that empowering others and seeing others do well could be so satisfying". Currently Khalid Bey is a City Councilor for the City of Syracuse where he takes advantage of the opportunity to fulfill his passion to make the lives of others better. His previous works continues to win favor with readers. When ask what it is that he aspires to do more than all else, he replied "to understand and inspire". An insightful man, we are consistently reminded of his favorite quote is: "In order to change the world, all one has to do is change his mind."

Other books by Khalid El Bey

Available on:

www.khalidelbey.com

www.amazon.com

www.barnesandnoble.com

From My Eyes.......

www.ingramcontent.com/pod-product-compliance
Lightning Source LLC
Chambersburg PA
CBHW060902280326
41934CB00007B/1151